Imray
UPPER RIVER
GREAT OUSE
Bedford to Pope's Corner

Compiled with the assistance of the
Great Ouse Boating Association Ltd

Imray Laurie Norie & Wilson Ltd
St Ives Cambridgeshire England

Published by
Imray, Laurie, Norie & Wilson Ltd
Wych House, St Ives, Huntingdon,
Cambridgeshire, PE17 4BT, England
☎ (01480) 462114 *Fax* (01480) 496109
1996

Cartography based on Ordnance Survey maps with the permission of the Controller HM Stationery Office. Crown Copyright reserved.

British Library Cataloguing in Publication Data.
A catalogue record for this book is available from the British Library.

ISBN 0 85288 364 1

CAUTION
Every effort has been taken to ensure accuracy of this book. It contains selected information and thus is not definitive and does not include all known information on the subject in hand. The author and publisher believe that its selection is a useful aid to prudent navigation but the safety of a vessel depends ultimately on the judgement of the navigator who should assess all information, published or unpublished, available to him.
    The text has been reproduced from the Environment Agency's *Navigations in the Anglian Region,* with permission.

KEY TO SYMBOLS
Fuel 🛢
Water ⚓
General Store GS
Post office ✉
Telephone ☎
Early closing E.C
Fish and chips F&C
Overhead cables with height in metres
Moorings

AW	Anglian Water
EA	Environment Agency
GOBA	Great Ouse Boating Association
U/S	upstream
D/S	downstream
M	Miles
km	kilometres
	Ouse Valley Way (footpath)

Note
Levels of lock cills and navigation levels are referred to a datum of 30·5m (100ft) below Ordnance Datum Newlyn.

Scale
1:21,120
3" to 1 mile
7·75cm to 1km

Printed in Great Britain by
Imray Laurie Norie & Wilson Ltd

Contents

The River Great Ouse

This atlas covers the upper part of the River Great Ouse above Popes Corner near Stretham up to the head of navigation above Bedford. The Lower Ouse & Cam is covered in a separate publication, the *The Rivers Cam and Lower Great Ouse* which embraces the area below Popes Corner including the tributary rivers. The Middle Level navigations are covered in a map of the *Middle Level* and the River Nene is also covered in a separate publication.

River Great Ouse rises in Northamptonshire and passes through various towns including Bedford, the market towns of St Neots, Huntingdon and St Ives. The cathedral city of Ely and the town of Littleport are the most important in the lower section. Cambridge is accessible from the River Cam. The Ouse eventually reaches the sea after flowing for some 75 miles, at King's Lynn on the Wash.

The river is navigable from Bedford to the sea but effectively river boats should not attempt the passage below Denver Sluice from which it is tidal and dangerous. The River Great Ouse and its associated waterways provides an extensive area for leisure boating and via the Middle Level drains it is linked to the River Nene. That river in turn provides access at Northampton to the Grand Union Canal and the rest of England's inland waterway system.

The River Great Ouse is essential to the drainage system of the Fens and its function as a navigation is affected by its use in controlling flooding. One of the key elements in the drainage system is Denver Sluice which is the largest structure of its kind in England. The history of draining the Fens is a long and interesting one and it is sufficient to point out here that many of the tributaries of the Great Ouse, in particular the new Bedford River, are artificial. Some of the drains were made as early as the seventeenth century and several pre date that time.

BOAT LICENSING AND REGISTRATION

All craft using the River Great Ouse and associated waterways are obliged to hold an up to date river licence.

Details of regional requirements for the registration and licensing of craft to use the Rivers Cam and Ouse and associated EA-controlled waterways are available from:

The Environment Agency
   Anglian Region
Kingfisher House
Goldhay Way
Orton Goldhay
Peterborough PE2 0ZR
☎ (01733) 371811

Boat owners navigating recreational waterways within EA Anglian Region should acquaint themselves with the following legislation, copies of which can be obtained from the NRA at the above address.

The Recreational Waterways (Registration) Byelaws 1979

The Recreational Waterways (General) Byelaws 1980

Upper River Great Ouse dimensions and distances

The River Ouse is now navigable from Earith to Bedford. At minimum levels there is, generally speaking, a minimum depth of 1·35m on the lower section of river, with the exception of a length of about 1·2km above Brownshill Staunch, where the depth may be only 0·9m. The upper section has a minimum depth of 1·2m except where shoaling may occur downstream of structures. The following table gives the particulars in regard to the locks, the levels being referred to are Ordnance Datum Newlyn. The headroom under bridges refers to normal navigation level and it is, of course, reduced when flood water is passing down the river.

Distances from Pope's Corner
Earth 11M 11·75km
Huntingdon 24M 38·5km
St Neots 34M 53km
Bedford 49M 77·25km
Waterbeach 8M 12·75km (Cam)
Cambridge 13M 21km (Cam)
Denver 19M 30·75km (Ely Ouse)
Littleport 9M 14·5km (Ely Ouse)
Ely 3M 4·75km (Ely Ouse)

Bedford Lock
Cill level u/s 23·29m d/s 22·59m
Draught 1·1m
Length 29·7m
Width 3·3m
Headroom Footbridge 1·1m. Vertical lift gate 2·05m

Cardington Lock
Cill level u/s22·17m d/s 20·83m
Draught 1·15m
Length 28·5m
Width 3·15m
Headroom Bridge.2·75m. Vertical lift gate 2·75m

Castle Mill Lock
Cill level u/s 19·8m d/s 18·0m
Draught 1·2m
Length 29·5m
Width 4·0m
Headroom Bridge 4·3m

Willington Lock
Cill level u/s 17·3m d/s 16·0m
Draught 1·3m min
Length 29·5m
Width 4·0m
Headroom Footbridge 4·06m

Barford Lock
Cill level u/s 16·0m d/s 14·8m
Draught 1·2m
Length 29·5m
Width 4·0m
Headroom Footbridge 4·55m

Roxton Lock
Cill level u/s 14·7m d/s 13·9m
Draught 1·15m
Length 26·0m
Width 4·0m
Headroom Bridge 2·75m

Eaton Socon Lock
Cill level u/s 13·08m d/s 11·95m
Draught 1·6m
Length 31·5m
Width 3·4m
3·2 at 1·2m draught at d/s end of lock
Headroom Gates 2·7m

St Neots Lock
Cill level u/s 11·40m d/s 10·13m
Draught 1·05m
Length 32·9m
Width 3·3m
Headroom Lock gates approx 3·7m

Offord Lock
Cill level u/s 9·60m d/s 8·69m
Draught 1·2m
Length 30·5m
Width 3·4m

Brampton Lock
Cill level u/s 8·29m d/s 7·59m
Draught 1·45m
Length 31·7m
Width 3·4m
3·25m at 1·2m draught
Headroom Lock gates approx 2·6m

Godmanchester Lock
Cill level u/s 7·42m d/s 6·66m
Draught 1·05m
Length 30·5m
Width 4·0m
Headroom Footbridge (at d/s level) 3·0m.
Lock gates approx 2·95m

Houghton Lock
Cill level u/s 6·16m d/s 4·42m
Draught 1·5m
Length 27·5m
Width 3·65m
Headroom Footbridge and gate 2·75m

Hemingford Lock
Cill level u/s 4·8m d/s 3·28m
Draught 1·5m
Length 28·0m
Width 3·85m
Headroom Footbridge (at d/s level) 2·75m.
Lock gates approx 2·75m

St Ives Lock
Cill level u/s 2·56m d/s 2·35m
Draught 0·95m
Length 31·3m
Width 3·35m
Headroom Lock guillotine approx 4·25m

Brownshill Lock
Cill level u/s 0·2m d/s 0·3m
Draught 1·5m
Length 30·8m
Width 4·0m
Headroom Footbridges (at u/s level) 3·4m. Lock gates approx (dependent on d/s level) 3·05m

Hermitage Lock, Earith
Cill level 100·0m
Length 30·5m
Draught 1·5m
Width 4·0m
Headroom Bridge 4·25m at 101·5m

Headroom at Normal Water Level

	Hrm
St Ives New Bridge	4·09m
St Ives Town Bridge	2·66m
Hemingford Lock Bridge	3·28m
Huntingdon Town Bridge (large arch)	3·35m
Railway Bridge approx	4·75m
Offord Lock Road Bridge	2·46m
St Neots Paper Mill Bridge	2·87m
St Neots Town Bridge	2·77m
Eaton Socon Lock Footbridge	2·74m
Tempsford New Road Bridge	3·65m
Tempsford Old Road Bridge	3·05m
Barford Bridge (two navigation arches)	2·97m
(UP arch width 4·0m)	
(DOWN arch width 3·5m)	
Goldington Railway Bridge (disused)	2·64m
Road and Pipe Bridge	2·74m
Bedford Marina Entrance Footbridge	2·74m
Railway Bridge	2·29m
Footbridge	2·90m
Bedford Inner Relief Road Bridge	2·69m
Footbridge	2·13m

Normal retention levels – Brownshill to Bedford

Brownshill u/s 3·17m d/s 1·83m (average – have recorded as low as 1·10m)
St Ives u/s 5·05m d/s 3·32m (in low flow period)

Hemingford u/s 6·34m d/s 5·10m
Houghton u/s 7·77m d/s6·40m
Godmanchester u/s 9·02m d/s 7·89m
Brampton u/s 9·84m d/s 9·05m
Offord u/s 11·13m d/s 9·90m
St Neots u/s 13·56m d/s 11·22m
(depends on Grafham pumping)
Eaton Socon u/s 15·01m d/s 13·59m
Roxton u/s 15·90m d/s 15·10m
Great Barford u/s 17·15m d/s 16·00m
Willington u/s 19·05m d/s 17·30m
Castle Mills u/s 21·9m d/s 19·2m
Cardington u/s 23·7m d/s 22·0m
Bedford u/s 24·8m d/s 23·7m

BOAT CLUBS AND MARINAS ON THE GREAT OUSE

Annesdale Marine, Annesdale Dock, Ely, Cambridgeshire ☎ (01353) 665420

Barford Boat Yard, New Road, Great Barford, Bedfordshire ☎ (01234) 870401

Bedford Boat Club, Brickhill, Bedford MK41 7XQ ☎ (01234) 34484

Bedford Boat Hire, 45A St Cuthberts Street, Bedford ☎ (01234) 212300

St Neots Marina, St Neots, Huntingdon, Cambridgeshire ☎ (01480) 472411

Bridge Boatyard, Ely, Cambridgeshire ☎ (01353) 663726

The Buckden Marina, Buckden, Huntingdon, Cambridgeshire ☎ (01480) 810355

Cambridge Motor Boat Club, Waterbeach, Cambridgeshire ☎ (01223) 860149

Carters Boatyard, Mill Road Buckden, Huntingdon, Cambridgeshire ☎ (01480) 811503

Crosshall Marine, Crosshall Road, St Neots, Huntingdon, Cambridgeshire ☎ (01480) 472763

Daylock Marine, Hartford Road, Wyton, Huntingdon, Cambridgeshire ☎ (01480) 455898

Daymond Hire Boats, 4 Spruce Road, Clackclose Park, Downham Market ☎ (01366) 383618

Denver Cruising Club, Old Ferry Boat Inn, Southery, Norfolk ☎ (01353) 76310

C D Elbrow Marine, Stretham, Cambridgeshire ☎ (01223) 63692

Ely Marina, Waterside, Ely, Cambridgeshire ☎ (01353) 664622

C Fox (Boatbuilders), 10 Marina Drive, March, Cambridgeshire ☎ (01354) 52770

Great Ouse Boating Association Mrs B. Arnold (Sec), 23 Alfred Cope Road, Sandy, Bedfordshire SG19 1LX ☎ (01767) 681247

Great Ouse Boatbuilders and Operators Association, Mrs Synod (Sec), Fox's Boatyard, 10 Marina Drive, March, Cambridgeshire PE15 0AY ☎ (01354) 52770

Hartford Marina, Hartford Road, Wyton, Huntingdon, Cambridgeshire ☎ (01480) 454677

Hermitage Marina, Earith, Huntingdon, Cambridgeshire ☎ (01487) 840994

Huntingdon Boat Haven, Godmanchester, Huntingdon, Cambridgeshire ☎(01480) 411977

Huntingdon Marine and Leisure, Godmanchester, Huntingdon, Cambridgeshire ☎ (01480) 413517

Inland Waterways Association, Mr J Davis (Sec), Dept of Anatomy, Cambridge University, Cambridge ☎ (01223) 333775

Isleham Marina, Fenbank, Isleham, Cambridgeshire ☎ (01638)780663

L. H. Jones & Son (Boatbuilders) Limited, The Boathaven, St Ives, Huntingdon, Cambridgeshire ☎ (01480) 494040

Kelpie Marine, Al Roxton, Bedford MK44 3DS ☎ (01234) 870249

Littleport Boat Haven, Litteport, Ely, Cambridgeshire ☎ (01353) 861969

Norman Cole Marine, Upware, Ely, Cambridgeshire ☎ (01223) 860528

Ouse Valley River Club, Mr A. Downing, 8 The Harriers, Sandy, Bedfordshire SG19 2TF ☎ (01462) 679850

Pike & Eel Marina, Overcote Road, Needingworth, Cambridgeshire ☎ (01767) 683538

Priory Marina, Barkers Lane, Bedford MK41 9RL ☎ (01234) 351931

Purvis Marine, Hartford Road, Huntingdon, Cambridgeshire ☎ (01480) 453628

Quiet Waters Boat Haven, Earith, Huntingdon, Cambridgeshire ☎ (01487) 842154

River Mill, School Lane, Eaton Socon St Neots, Huntingdon, Cambridgeshire ☎ (01480) 473456

Twenty Pence Marina, Twenty Pence Road, Wilburton, Ely, Cambridgeshire ☎ (01954) 51118

Two Tees Boatyard, 70 Water Street, Cambridge ☎ (01223) 65597

Upware Marine (Trebleways) Ltd, Upware, Ely, Cambridgeshire ☎ (01353) 721930

West View Marina, Earith, Huntingdon, Cambridgeshire ☎ (01487) 841627

Boatyards
Boat Deliveries, St Ives Pilotage Company ☎ (01480) 462555

PUBLIC LAUNCHING SITES
River Ouse
St Neots by rowing club
Godmanchester (The Causeway)
Huntingdon (D/S of Purvis Marine by Rowing Club)
St Ives (in quay D/S of bridge)
Ely (Waterside)
Denver
Tidal River Ouse
King's Lynn Common Staithe Quay

TOILET PUMP-OUT SERVICES
River Ouse
River Mill, River Mill, School Lane, Eaton Socon, St Neots, Cambridgeshire ☎ (01480) 473456
Hartford Marina, Hartford Road, Wyton, Huntingdon, Cambridgeshire ☎ (01480) 454677
Hermitage Marina, Earith, Huntingdon, Cambridgeshire ☎ (01487) 840994

GOBA MOORINGS
Offord
Adjacent to the landing stage on right hand bank below lock.

Mailers Meadow
LH bank between Buckden Marina and Brampton lock.

Brampton
LH bank between Brampton Mill and railway bridge.

Hemingford Meadow
RH bank between Sleeping Waters and Hemingford Grey.

Noble's Field
LH bank between Hemingford lock and St Ives.

Pike & Eel, Overcote Ferry
LH Bank immediately prior to entrance to Pike & Eel Marina. 200m in length.

Aldreth Drain (Old West)
LH bank 200m before high bridge.

Lazy Otter (Old West)
LH bank 130m downstream of public house moorings.

EA AND LOCAL COUNCIL SHORT STAY MOORINGS (48 HOURS)

River Ouse
(Old West River)
Streatham Engine Bridge
St Ives – The Waits
St Ives – town centre and Dolphin Pool
Hemingford Grey
Houghton
Huntingdon
Godmanchester
St Neots
Tempsford
Great Barford Bridge
Great Barford Old Mills
Bedford

EA ANGLIAN REGION. DISTRICT OFFICES AND THEIR AREAS
Telephone numbers refer to office hours

Central Area
Bromholme Lane, Brampton, Huntingdon
☎ (01480) 414581

Bedford Ouse
Kempston to Earith
EA Bedford
☎ (01234) 262622

Note
Outside office hours contact ☎ (01733) 371811 in either case emergencies will be dealt with immediately. If a resolution of the problem is likely to be delayed, the caller will be contacted and appraised of the situation.

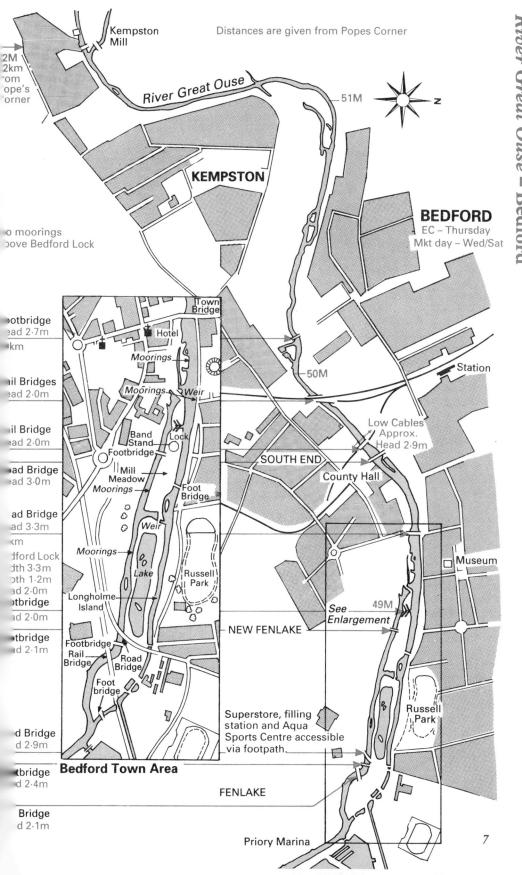

Kempston
Mill

Distances are given from Popes Corner

River Great Ouse

51M

2M
2km
rom
ope's
orner

KEMPSTON

BEDFORD
EC – Thursday
Mkt day – Wed/Sat

o moorings
bove Bedford Lock

Town
Bridge

otbridge
ead 2·7m
km

Hotel

Moorings

Station

Moorings   Weir

50M

il Bridges
ead 2·0m

il Bridge
ead 2·0m

Band
Stand   Lock

Low Cables
Approx.
Head 2·9m

ad Bridge
ead 3·0m

Footbridge
Mill
Meadow

SOUTH END

Moorings
Foot
Bridge

County Hall

ad Bridge
ad 3·3m
km

Weir

dford Lock
th 3·3m
th 1·2m
ad 2·0m
otbridge
ad 2·0m

Moorings

Lake   Russell
Park

Museum

Longholme
Island

*See
Enlargement*

49M

tbridge
ad 2·1m

Footbridge
Rail
Bridge   Road
Bridge

NEW FENLAKE

Foot
bridge

Superstore, filling
station and Aqua
Sports Centre accessible
via footpath.

Russell
Park

d Bridge
d 2·9m

Bedford Town Area

tbridge
d 2·4m

FENLAKE

Bridge
d 2·1m

Priory Marina

7

GOLDINGTON

Bedford
Boat Club

Barns
Restaurant
☎ (01234)
270044

Weir

48M

Priory
Country
Park

Priory Marina
(All facilities)
☎ (01234) 351931

*Canoe
Slalom
Course*

To Cardington
1 mile

Weir

Fishing
Lake

New Cut

Cardington Lock
Width 3·1m
Depth 1·15m
Head 2·7m
47M 74km

*Sluice
Gate*

*Navigation
Channel*

The
Green

Rail & Road Bridges
Head 2·6m

Sewage Works

Distances are from Pope's Corner

46M

N

Railway (disused)

Castle Mill Lock
Width 4·0m
Depth 1·2m
Head 4·3m
(Fall 2·7m)
44½M 72km

Risinghoe
Castle
(Motte)

Sluices

Bedford
Castle Mill
Airfield

Castle
Dairy
Farm

New Bedford Bypass

NOTE
There are no moorings
between the old lock
above Great Barford
and Cardington Lock.

*River
Great Ouse*

45M

10·0m

New Bedford Bypass Bridge
Head 6.2m

Plantations

Howbury
Hall

WILLINGTON

10·0m

44M

Water
End

Great
Dairy
Farm

WILLINGTON

44M

Gadsey Brook

A428

Willington Lock
Width 4·0m
Depth 1·4m Head 4·0m

Weir

Footbridge
42M 67·5km

Mill Farm

10·0m
43M

Old Lock
Navigation Prohibited

Overnight Moorings

Old Sluice
Navigation Prohibited

Footbridge
Head 4·4m

oad Bridge

GREAT BARFORD

Golden Cross PH (Food)
☎ (01234) 870437

Anchor PH (Food)
☎ (01234) 870864

ead u/s arch 3·2m

Bridge Farm

(GS, PO, ☎)

Vidth u/s arch 3·8m

ead d/s arch 3·0m at centre

Vidth d/s arch 4·0m

42M

Public Moorings and Slipway

D. Garrard Boatbuilder

reat Barford Lock
Vidth 4·0m
epth 1·3m
ead 4·5m
ootbridge

Weir ☎ (01234) 870401

To Blunham 1 mile

River Great Ouse

Great Barford House

M 66km

41M

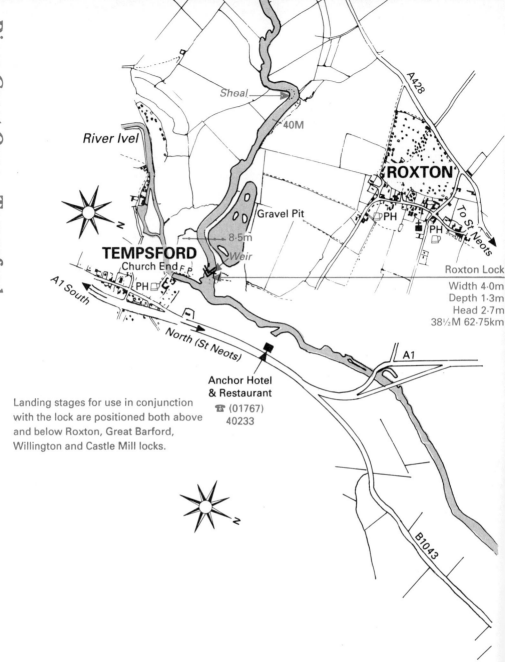

Sheal

40M

River Ivel

ROXTON

A428

Gravel Pit

PH

PH

To St Neots

8·5m

TEMPSFORD
Church End F.P.

Weir

A1 South

PH

North (St Neots)

Roxton Lock
Width 4·0m
Depth 1·3m
Head 2·7m
38½M 62·75km

A1

B1043

Anchor Hotel
& Restaurant
☎ (01767)
40233

Landing stages for use in conjunction
with the lock are positioned both above
and below Roxton, Great Barford,
Willington and Castle Mill locks.

Distances are from Pope's Corner

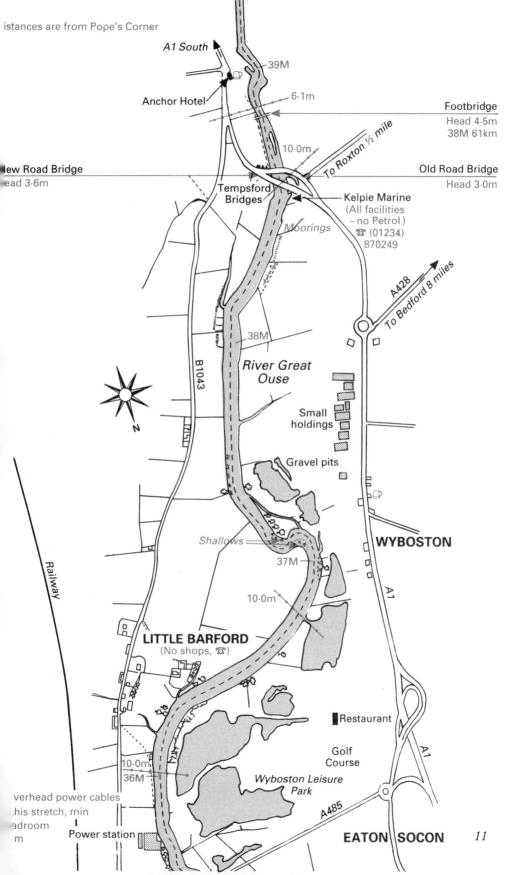

istances are from Pope's Corner

A1 South

39M

Anchor Hotel

6·1m

Footbridge
Head 4·5m
38M 61km

10·0m

To Roxton ½ mile

ew Road Bridge
ead 3·6m

Old Road Bridge
Head 3·0m

Tempsford
Bridges

Kelpie Marine
(All facilities
– no Petrol)
☎ (01234)
870249

Moorings

A428

To Bedford 8 miles

38M

B1043

*River Great
Ouse*

Small
holdings

N

Gravel pits

Shallows

WYBOSTON

37M

A1

10·0m

LITTLE BARFORD
(No shops, ☎)

Railway

Restaurant

Golf
Course

A1

10·0m
36M

*Wyboston Leisure
Park*

verhead power cables
his stretch, min
adroom
m

Power station

A485

EATON SOCON

11

Power
Station

New Road Bridge

A1

Cambridge

A428

Cables
Head 6·1m

EATON SOCON
(Public Houses)
(GS, ✉ , But ☎)

Weir

Eaton Socon Lock

Width 3·4m
Depth 1·6m
Head 2·5m
35M 54·7km

B1046

B1043

Sluices

Shallows to about 0·75m

River Mill Boats
(All facilities except
petrol)
☎ (01480) 473456

The Mill Tavern
Restaurant
☎ (01480) 219612

Ernulf
School

Cricket
Ground

Railway London – Peterborough

EA Moorings

Footbridge

Riverside
34M   Park

EYNESBURY

EATON FORD

PH

St Neots Bridge

ST NEOTS

St Neots Marina
(All facilities – no petrol)
☎ (01480) 472411

Old Falcon PH
☎ (01480) 472749

Old
Bridge Hotel

St Neots
RC

Moorings

Head 3·0m
33M 53km

Public water tap on stage
next hotel

To Cambridge
17 miles

Ouse Valley
River Club

Public moorings

Golf
course

B1043

Crosshall Marin
(All facilities
– no petrol)
☎ (01480) 472763

St Neots Station

River Kym

Islands
Common

33M

Navigable for sma
cruisers for about
1 mile

N

Road Bridge
Head 2·7m

Distances are from
Pope's Corner

Huntingdon

Sluices

Shallows to about 0·7m

10·0m

6·1m

Factory Bridg
Head 3·9

St Neots Loc
Width 3·5k
Head 3·0
Depth 1·1
32M 51·5k

Sewage
Works

32M

Paper
Mill

Paxton Park

*Shallow about
1·0m*

A1

6·1m
Gravel pit

**LITTLE
PAXTON**

12

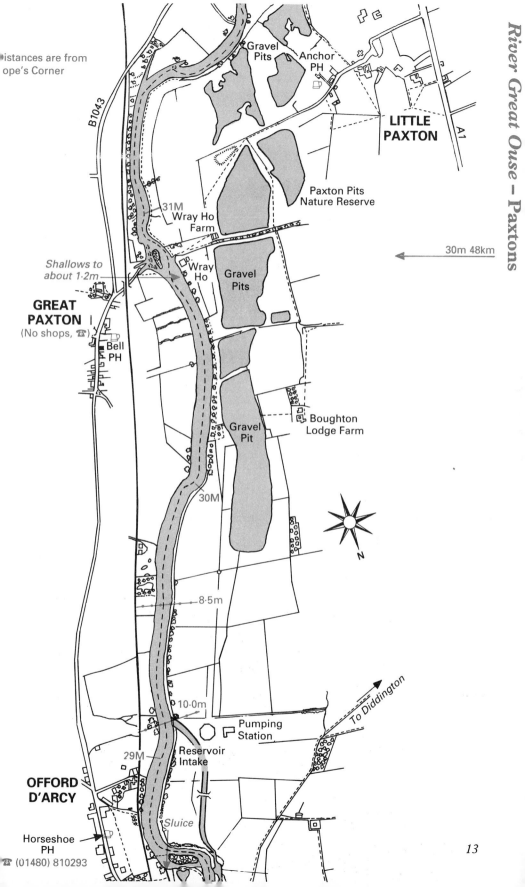

istances are from
ope's Corner

Gravel Pits

Anchor PH

LITTLE PAXTON

B1043

A1

Paxton Pits
Nature Reserve

31M

Wray Ho Farm

30m 48km

Shallows to about 1·2m

Wray Ho

Gravel Pits

GREAT PAXTON
(No shops, ☎)

Bell PH

Boughton Lodge Farm

Gravel Pit

30M

N

8·5m

To Diddington

10·0m

Pumping Station

29M

Reservoir Intake

OFFORD D'ARCY

Sluice

Horseshoe PH
☎ (01480) 810293

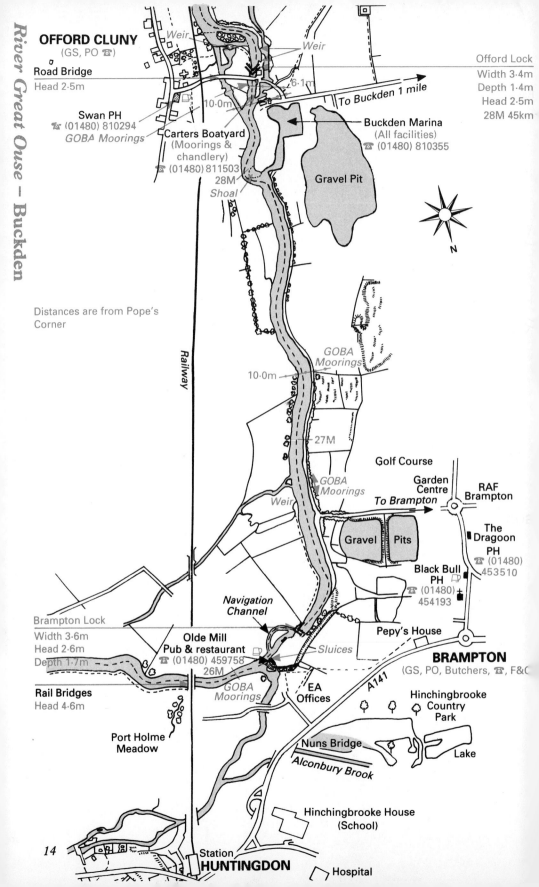

OFFORD CLUNY
(GS, PO ☎)

Weir

Weir

Road Bridge
Head 2·5m

6·1m

To Buckden 1 mile

Swan PH
☎ (01480) 810294
GOBA Moorings

10·0m

Buckden Marina
(All facilities)
☎ (01480) 810355

Carters Boatyard
(Moorings &
chandlery)
☎ (01480) 811503
28M
Shoal

Gravel Pit

N

Distances are from Pope's
Corner

Railway

*GOBA
Moorings*

10·0m

27M

Golf Course

*GOBA
Moorings*

Garden
Centre
To Brampton

RAF
Brampton

Weir

The
Dragoon
PH
☎ (01480)
453510

Gravel | Pits

Black Bull
PH
☎ (01480)
454193

Brampton Lock
Width 3·6m
Head 2·6m
Depth 1·7m

*Navigation
Channel*

Pepy's House

BRAMPTON
(GS, PO, Butchers, ☎, F&C

Olde Mill
Pub & restaurant
☎ (01480) 459758
26M

Sluices

Rail Bridges
Head 4·6m

*GOBA
Moorings*

EA
Offices

A141

Hinchingbrooke
Country
Park

Port Holme
Meadow

Nuns Bridge

Lake

Alconbury Brook

Hinchingbrooke House
(School)

14

Station
HUNTINGDON

Hospital

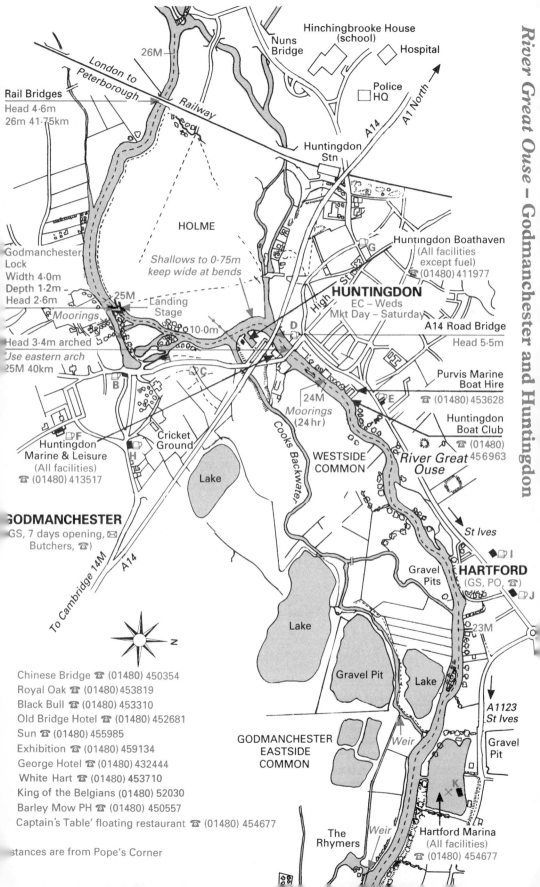

Hinchingbrooke House (school)

Nuns Bridge

Hospital

26M

Police HQ

London to Peterborough Railway

A14

A1 North

Rail Bridges
Head 4·6m
26m 41·75km

Huntingdon Stn

HOLME

Huntingdon Boathaven
(All facilities
except fuel)
☎ (01480) 411977

G

Godmanchester Lock
Width 4·0m
Depth 1·2m
Head 2·6m

*Shallows to 0·75m
keep wide at bends*

25M

HUNTINGDON
EC – Weds
Mkt Day – Saturday

High St

Moorings

Landing Stage

10·0m

D

A14 Road Bridge
Head 5·5m

Head 3·4m arched
Use eastern arch
25M 40km

B

C

24M

E

Purvis Marine
Boat Hire
☎ (01480) 453628

*Moorings
(24 hr)*

Huntingdon
Boat Club
☎ (01480)
456963

F

Huntingdon
Marine & Leisure
(All facilities)
☎ (01480) 413517

H

Cricket
Ground

Lake

Cooks Backwater

WESTSIDE
COMMON

*River Great
Ouse*

GODMANCHESTER
GS, 7 days opening, ✉
Butchers, ☎)

To Cambridge 14M

A14

St Ives

I

Gravel
Pits

HARTFORD
(GS, PO, ☎)

J

Lake

Gravel Pit

Lake

23M

N

*A1123
St Ives*

Chinese Bridge ☎ (01480) 450354
Royal Oak ☎ (01480) 453819
Black Bull ☎ (01480) 453310
Old Bridge Hotel ☎ (01480) 452681
Sun ☎ (01480) 455985
Exhibition ☎ (01480) 459134
George Hotel ☎ (01480) 432444
White Hart ☎ (01480) 453710
King of the Belgians (01480) 52030
Barley Mow PH ☎ (01480) 450557
Captain's Table' floating restaurant ☎ (01480) 454677

Distances are from Pope's Corner

GODMANCHESTER
EASTSIDE
COMMON

Weir

Gravel
Pit

K

The
Rhymers

Weir

Hartford Marina
(All facilities)
☎ (01480) 454677

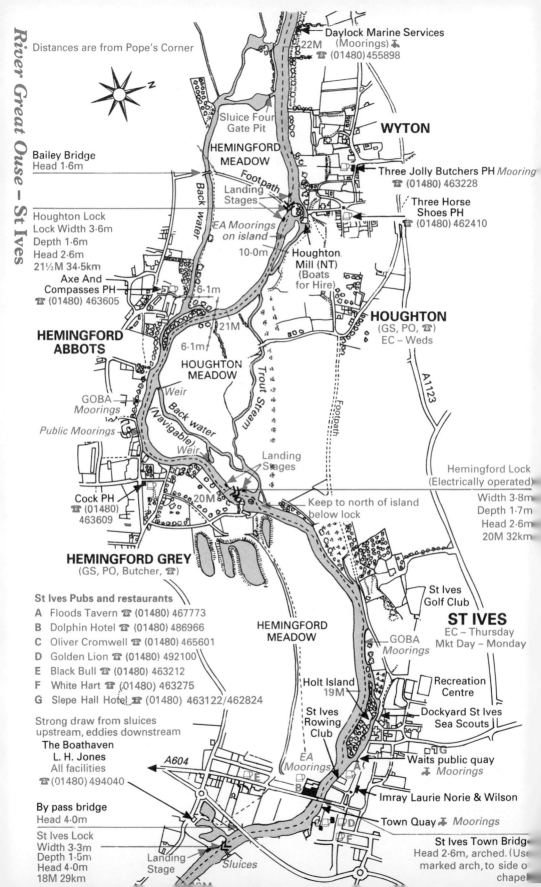

Distances are from Pope's Corner

N

Daylock Marine Services
(Moorings) ⚓
22M ☎ (01480) 455898

WYTON

Sluice Four
Gate Pit

**HEMINGFORD
MEADOW**

Bailey Bridge
Head 1·6m

Footpath

Landing
Stages

Three Jolly Butchers PH *Mooring*
☎ (01480) 463228

Three Horse
Shoes PH
☎ (01480) 462410

Houghton Lock
Lock Width 3·6m
Depth 1·6m
Head 2·6m
21½M 34·5km

*EA Moorings
on island*

10·0m

Houghton
Mill (NT)
(Boats
for Hire)

Axe And
Compasses PH
☎ (01480) 463605

6·1m

HOUGHTON
(GS, PO, ☎)
EC – Weds

A1123

**HEMINGFORD
ABBOTS**

21M

6·1m

**HOUGHTON
MEADOW**

Weir

GOBA
Moorings

Back water
(Navigable)

Trout Stream

Footpath

Public Moorings

Weir

Landing
Stages

Hemingford Lock
(Electrically operated)
Width 3·8m
Depth 1·7m
Head 2·6m
20M 32km

Cock PH
☎ (01480)
463609

20M

Keep to north of island
below lock

St Ives
Golf Club

HEMINGFORD GREY
(GS, PO, Butcher, ☎)

ST IVES
EC – Thursday
Mkt Day – Monday

St Ives Pubs and restaurants
A Floods Tavern ☎ (01480) 467773
B Dolphin Hotel ☎ (01480) 486966
C Oliver Cromwell ☎ (01480) 465601
D Golden Lion ☎ (01480) 492100
E Black Bull ☎ (01480) 463212
F White Hart ☎ (01480) 463275
G Slepe Hall Hotel ☎ (01480) 463122/462824

**HEMINGFORD
MEADOW**

GOBA
Moorings

Recreation
Centre

Holt Island
19M

Dockyard St Ives
Sea Scouts

Strong draw from sluices
upstream, eddies downstream

The Boathaven
L. H. Jones
All facilities
☎ (01480) 494040

St Ives
Rowing
Club

*EA
Moorings*

G

Waits public quay
⚓ *Moorings*

A604

A

Imray Laurie Norie & Wilson

B

By pass bridge
Head 4·0m

D

Town Quay ⚓ *Moorings*

F

St Ives Lock
Width 3·3m
Depth 1·5m
Head 4·0m
18M 29km

Landing
Stage

Sluices

St Ives Town Bridge
Head 2·6m, arched. (Use
marked arch, to side of
chapel)

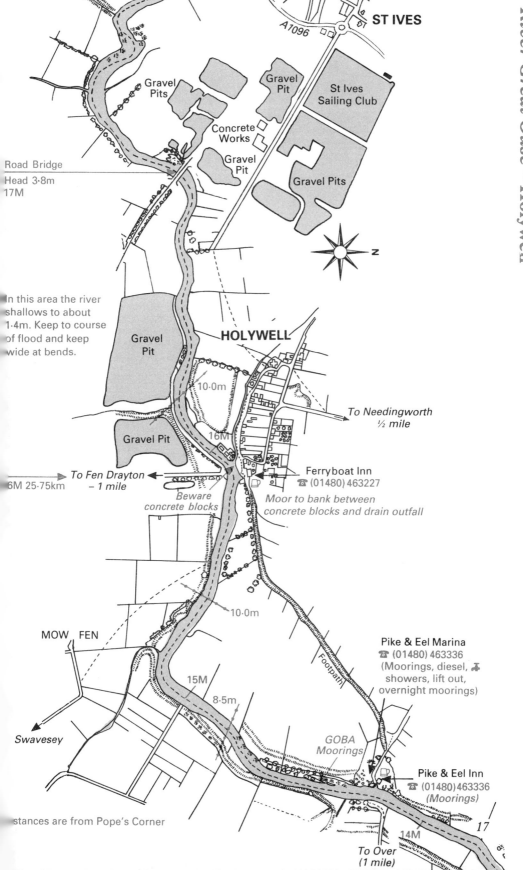

ST IVES

A1096

Gravel Pits

Gravel Pit

Concrete Works

Gravel Pit

St Ives Sailing Club

Gravel Pits

Road Bridge
Head 3·8m
17M

In this area the river shallows to about 1·4m. Keep to course of flood and keep wide at bends.

Gravel Pit

HOLYWELL

10·0m

16M

Gravel Pit

To Needingworth ½ mile

26M 25·75km

To Fen Drayton – 1 mile

Beware concrete blocks

Ferryboat Inn
☎ (01480) 463227

Moor to bank between concrete blocks and drain outfall

10·0m

MOW FEN

Pike & Eel Marina
☎ (01480) 463336
(Moorings, diesel, showers, lift out, overnight moorings)

15M

8·5m

Swavesey

Footpath

GOBA Moorings

Pike & Eel Inn
☎ (01480) 463336
(Moorings)

17

Distances are from Pope's Corner

14M

To Over (1 mile)

14M

Distances are from Pope's Corner

Sluices

To St Ives

A1123

Brownshill Lock
Width 4·0m
Depth 1·4m
Head U/S 3·3m
Head D/S Gate 3·0m
13M 21km

Landing
Stages

OUSE FEN

Trinity College
Farm

THIS SECTION IS TIDAL
Take care on mooring, during the summer season the rise
and fall is only about 0·3m but at spring tides it may be
about 0·75m. Heights are also affected by local rains.
Measurements shown are for normal average conditions.
Consult the lock keeper

EARITH
(GS, PO,
Butchers, ☎)
E.cl. – Wed

N

Westview Marinas Ltd
(All facilities. Provisions, diesel, water
showers, lift out, overnight moorings)
☎ (01487) 841627

Quiet Waters Boat Haven
Moorings only
☎ (01487) 842154

Crown PH
Landing Stage
overnight moorings)
☎ (01487) 841442

Fixed
Sluice

Old
Bedford
River

Riverview Inn
(Water, food, overnight moorings)

Hermitage Lock (01487) 841548

Depth 1·5m
Width 4·0m
Head 3·4m
11M 17·75km

Road bridge across lock restricts
headroom if Earith Reach is high with
tide or flood.

Landing Stages

10·0m

10·0m

New Bedford River (Tidal)

Hermitage Marina
(All facilities)
☎ (01487)
840994

18

To Ely 12 miles
A1123

See maps
Rivers Cam and Lower Ouse
for details of tidal rivers

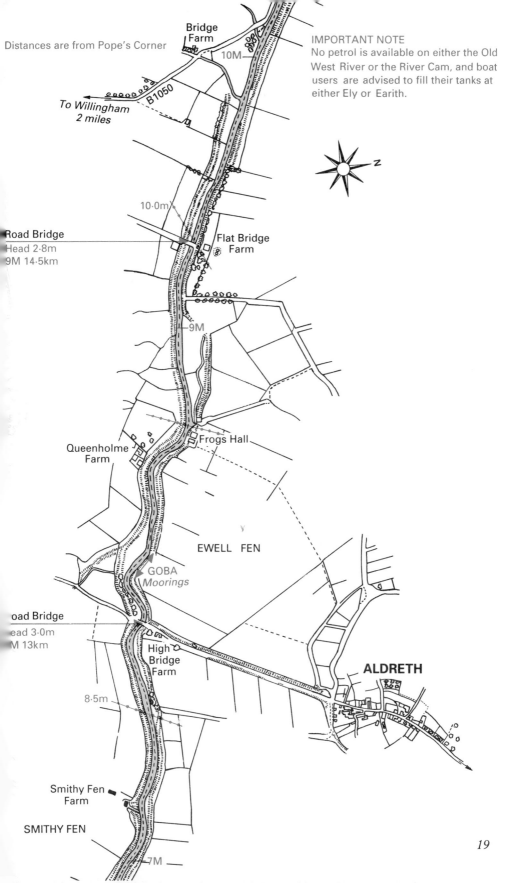

Distances are from Pope's Corner

Bridge
Farm

10M

To Willingham
2 miles

B1050

IMPORTANT NOTE
No petrol is available on either the Old
West River or the River Cam, and boat
users are advised to fill their tanks at
either Ely or Earith.

N

10·0m

Road Bridge
Head 2·8m
9M 14·5km

Flat Bridge
Farm

9M

Queenholme
Farm

Frogs Hall

EWELL   FEN

GOBA
Moorings

oad Bridge
ead 3·0m
M 13km

High
Bridge
Farm

ALDRETH

8·5m

Smithy Fen
Farm

SMITHY FEN

7M

19

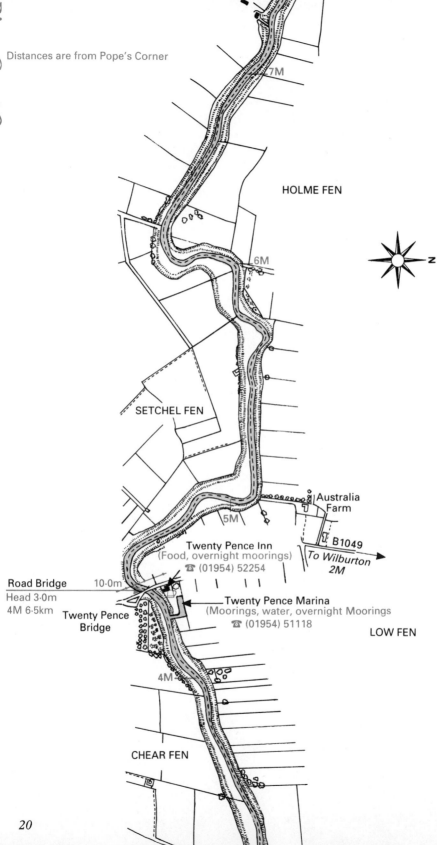

Distances are from Pope's Corner

7M

HOLME FEN

6M

SETCHEL FEN

5M

Australia
Farm

B1049
To Wilburton
2M

Twenty Pence Inn
(Food, overnight moorings)
☎ (01954) 52254

Road Bridge   10·0m
Head 3·0m
4M 6·5km
          Twenty Pence
          Bridge

Twenty Pence Marina
(Moorings, water, overnight Moorings
☎ (01954) 51118

LOW FEN

4M

CHEAR FEN

Distances are from Pope's Corner

To nbridge

Willow Grange Farm

Chear Fen Farm

10·0m

3M

Boat Repairs C. D. Elbrow
☎ (01223) 63692

Grange Farm

A10

Stretham Ferry Bridge

GOBA *Moorings*

Lazy Otter PH
⚓ Food, (overnight moorings)
☎ (01353) 649780

New Road Bridge
Head 3·0m
3M 5km

Old Road Bridge
Head 2·9m

10·0m

2M

lew Concrete oad Bridge
lead 3·3m

Bridge House Wooden Bridge
EA *48 hr Moorings*

Stretham Engine

8·5m

STRETHAM
(Shops, PO, ☎)

To Ely
A10

Green End

Stow Bridge Farm

lew Concrete oad Bridge
lead 3·2m

A1123

8·5m

1M

21

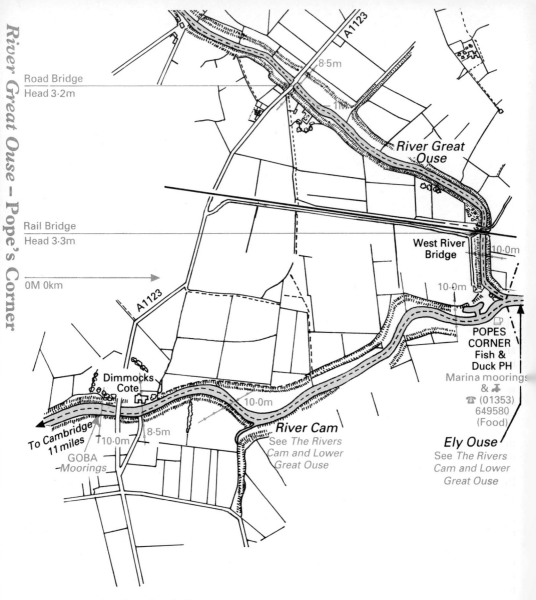

Road Bridge
Head 3·2m

Rail Bridge
Head 3·3m

0M 0km

A1123

A1123

8·5m

1m

River Great
Ouse

West River
Bridge

10·0m

10·0m

POPES
CORNER
Fish &
Duck PH
Marina moorings
& ⚓
☎ (01353)
649580
(Food)

Dimmocks
Cote

10·0m

River Cam
See *The Rivers
Cam and Lower
Great Ouse*

To Cambridge
11 miles

8·5m

10·0m

GOBA
Moorings

Ely Ouse
See *The Rivers
Cam and Lower
Great Ouse*

Distances are given from Pope's Corner

Local Notes

THE OUSE VALLEY

These notes have been based on information given in *Ouse Valley Trail* published by the Huntingdonshire District Council Planning Department with permission.

The River Great Ouse flows for 25 miles through Huntingdonshire. The riverside villages of the Ouse valley are some of the prettiest in the country, set amongst quiet backwaters and lush meadowlands. To compliment these attractions the area offers a rich heritage of historical sites and fine buildings.

The Great Ouse has helped to determine the pattern of development in Huntingdonshire. In early times settlements were established at crossing places or ancient fording points. Later, the river became a means of communication and of strategic importance to the invading Danes in the 9th and 10th centuries, and also for the Normans, who were responsible for the castle earthworks on the riverside, to guard important river crossings.

During the 16th century the course of the river to the sea was shortened when the then Duke of Bedford bought the drainage rights and cut the Old and New Bedford Rivers in 1631 and 1651 respectively. The River Ouse became an important defensive barrier during the Civil War period, with many of its bridges being fortified.

The valley boasts several fine manor houses, including the former stately home of Hinchingbrooke House and a wealth of interesting churches. Whilst not every village had its own mill, watermills were once a common site throughout the Ouse valley but, many mentioned in the Domesday Book have since disappeared. It was to these places that the local people would bring corn to be ground on payment of a toll to the lord of the manor. Houghton Mill, (now in the ownership of the National Trust), is one of the few remaining watermills, but the mill buildings of Offord and Buckden, Little Paxton and Brampton, (complete with waterwheel), can still be seen.

The Great Ouse was responsible for the industrial and commercial activity in some settlements, being navigable throughout the county from St Neots in the south to Earith in the east and then to the Wash via Denver in Norfolk. Many of the towns' brewing, paper-making, timber-processing activities still flourish today, although the river as a line of communication diminished after the opening of the Great Northern Railway in 1850.

Today, the river traffic is largely for pleasure and there are many points from which boats can be hired for an unrivalled view of the Great Ouse. The stretch of river between Huntingdon and St Ives ranks as one of the most pleasant reaches of any river navigation in England.

BEDFORD

Bedford, the county town was granted its charter in 1166 by Henry II. John Howard (1726–1790), the prison reformer was born here, and John Bunyon (1628–1688) wrote Pilgrim's Progress (published in 1678) while imprisoned in the county gaol. Bunyon was born a couple of miles outside Bedford at Harrowden.

The river is navigable to Kempston Mill but many cruisers are restricted by head room, including the lock, above Mill Meadow. At Mill Meadow there is public mooring although it is some distance from the main shopping centre. The town has many pubs, restaurants as well as an art gallery, museum, amateur theatre, ten-pin bowling, cinema complex and modern swimming pool. These facilities are all within easy reach of the river. So too is the corn Exchange which offers a variety of live entertainment. The tourist information office ☎ (01234) 215226 is in St Paul's Square at the north end of the Town Bridge.

Market days are Wednesday and Saturday on the new market place in River Street.

ST NEOTS

Grew up around a Benedictine Priory in the 10th century alongside the river, which disappeared after the Dissolution in 1539. The impressive spire of 15th-century St Mary's Church is a feature of the town, whose industries of brewing, paper-making and timber processing were based on early river navigation. The huge market square, flanked by fine 18th-century and 19th-century buildings, including Paines old brewery (1831), is the historic setting for the weekly Thursday market. Here the Ouse is crossed by a modern road bridge, which replaced an earlier 17th-century stone bridge that was fortified, and in 1648 the scene of a battle during the Civil War. Here also is the riverside park, which is crossed by a network of paths with footbridges over small streams and backwaters.

EYNESBURY
Formerly a separate village but is now part of St Neots, being divided only by a small street known as Hen Brook. The road over the bridge leads past the 12th-century church of St Mary, whose Gothic tower can be seen from the attractive village green further on. The Coneygeare riverside park provides an ideal spot for viewing the river and gaining access to the main riverside park.

EATON SOCON
Part of modern St Neots, but was once a fording point fortified by the impressive ancient castle earthworks known as Castle Hills. Nearby is the recently renovated River Mill (1847) and its attractive Mill Race. The village lock-up stands at the roadside, immediately opposite the restored early 14th-century parish church of St Mary. Being situated on the Old Great North Road, Eaton Socon retains several old coaching inns and hostelries.

LITTLE PAXTON
A recently expanded settlement immediately north of St Neots. Formerly a hamlet, centred on the late 12th-century parish church of St James and Paxton Hall rebuilt in 1738, the large wooded grounds of Paxton Park separated this area from the mill buildings clustered around the river crossing to the south. Today, this stretch of the Ouse Valley has largely been transformed into a series of lakes by gravel workings which have been linked together by a network of recreational footpaths.

OFFORD CLUNY
The most northerly of the two Offord villages, which was once part of the Cluny Abbey estate in Burgandy between the 11th century and 15th century. The red

brick Manor House was not built, however, until 1704. Nearby is the former village school dated 1850, which bears an inscription above the entrance door dedicated to Dr. Newcome, who left a sum of money in 1763 to educate six poor children. The church of All Saints dates from the 13th century and has a footpath leading down to the railway and then onto the weirs on the river and the picturesque setting of the Offord and Buckden corn mill.

OFFORD D'ARCY
Separated only by a small street from Offord Cluny. A tall spire overlooks the long tree lined-driveway to the church of St Peter and the adjacent manor house. The medieval church, now redundant, contains 14th-century carvings and memorials to the Nailour family who built the manor house in 1613.

GREAT PAXTON
Lies beside the main King's Cross to Edinburgh railway line. At the northern end of the village is an attractive terrace of cottages that lead down to the highly interesting 'minster' church, (dated about 1050), with one of the rare aisled naves of the Saxon period still left in this country. Immediately to the south of the village is the steeply-sided Paxton Hill, which provides unrivalled views over the Ouse valley and the Paxton pits beyond.

BUCKDEN
An historic village beside the A1 and is famous for its great palace built by the Bishops of Lincoln. Set in splendid grounds remains the red-bricked 15th-century gatehouse, and the Great Tower where Catherine of Aragon was imprisoned by Henry VIII before being removed to Kimbolton Castle. Several bishops who stayed here have monuments in the adjoining parish church of St Mary, opposite the former Manor House. Buckden has several distinguished buildings which reflect its importance as a posting station on the old Great North Road, including the 16th-century Lion Hotel and the 18th-century George Hotel with its old forge.

BRAMPTON

Immediately west of Huntingdon and famous for its National Hunt Racecourse. Although the village has expanded rapidly in recent years, partly due to the presence of the RAF station in the former park, there is a large part of the old village left intact. The long and winding High Street leads past the small museum in the old forge to the attractive tree-lined village green at the far end. A footpath leads from the 13th-century church of St Mary's across open meadows and eventually onto the vast 300-acre meadow of Portholme. Close by is the 16th-century timber-framed Black Bull coaching inn, frequented by the famous diarist Samuel Pepys. On the road to Huntingdon, past the 18th-century stone obelisk, is Pepys' House (No 44), home of the Pepys family and where Samuel spent his childhood years.

GODMANCHESTER

Linked to Huntingdon by an ancient stone bridge (1332) across the River Ouse. In Roman times the town was an important fording point, with a formal pentagonal street pattern. Although one of the earliest boroughs to receive its charter from King John in 1214, it has however, the character of a village rather than a town. There are many attractions, including the 18th-century street frontage at the Causeway, providing a pleasant view across the Mill Pond at the famous Chinese Bridge (1827). From here a footpath leads across the mill race and the river to the vast Port Holme meadow.

HUNTINGDON

The former county town, is famous as the birth-place of Oliver Cromwell (1599-1658). Market Hill is the setting for the Saturday market and is flanked by the red-bricked Town Hall (1745) and the 15th-century All Saints Church. This also contains the Falcon Inn, which was used as a headquarters by Cromwell during the Civil War, and the Cromwell Museum. The town is linked to Godmanchester by an ancient stone bridge, guarded on the south bank by the former hosiery mill. The riverside park provides splendid views of the Ouse as it winds its way through the town.

HARTFORD

A former village, Hartford is now linked to Huntingdon on its eastern edge and can easily be reached by a footpath through the riverside park. The old part of the village has some notable buildings, including the 18th-century Hartford House and the 16th-century Manor House along Main Street. An attractive view of the riverside can be gained near the 12th-century church, which stands amidst picturesque cottages on the water's edge.

HEMINGFORD ABBOTS

Hemingford Abbots was once part of the Ramsey Abbey estate, which is clustered around the 13th-century church of St Margaret and the 16th-century Manor House opposite. The church, whose spire is a riverside landmark, also contains a Roman-Britain stone coffin which was found in a nearby field in 1889. There is also a popular footpath from the Black Bridge across the water meadows to Houghton Mill and two attractive meres in the parkland grounds of Hemingford Park Hall (1842-3).

HEMINGFORD GREY

The most easterly of the two attractive Hemingford villages. The waterside church of St James's provides one of the most memorable views of the Ouse, perched on the very edge of the river bank. It dates mainly from the 12th century to 14th century, although most of the spire was swept into the river in a gale in 1741. Several notable homes nearby include the moated Norman Manor House (1150), one of the oldest inhabited houses in England, once home of writer Lucy Boston but is not open to the public; the red-bricked former Rectory (1697) known as Hemingford Grey House, whose grounds contain one of Britain's largest plane trees, planted in 1702; and the mid 18th-century River House, home of the artist Dendy Sadler from 1900-1923.

HOUGHTON AND WYTON

Two charming villages linked together whose church spires dominate the landscape. Wyton has a 13th-century church with a 19th-century spire. Houghton has a famous 17th-century

Watermill of red-brick construction partly timber-framed and covered with weather boarding, set in an island location on quiet backwaters. The former village green area at Houghton contains the oldest timber framed house in the district, dated 1480; a Gothic village pump; and a bust of Potto Brown, an 19th-century philanthropist and once tenant of the Mill. There is also a pleasant meadowside walk along the Thicket footpath to St Ives.

ST IVES

St Ives is a lively town famous for it 15th-century chapel bridge and quayside which is a popular spot for boats to moor and from which to view the river. The Norris Museum and Library has an interesting local history collection. Market Hill provides the historic setting for the Monday, Friday and Bank Holiday markets. The 15th-century parish church with its soaring spire stands close to the old fording point to Hemingford Meadows.

HOLYWELL

Holywell is a small, picturesque village beyond Needingworth, set on the old bank of the Ouse know as the Front. An attractive row of timbered cottages stand close to the 13th-century church, whose tower was built of stone and came from Ramsey Abbey during the 16th-century and below which is the 'Holy Well' spring from which the village derives its name. The Old Ferry Boat Inn stands at the old ferry crossing point to the neighbouring village of Fen Drayton. A pleasant footpath walk (1½ miles) links with the Pike and Eel Inn, a similar crossing point downstream and beauty spot.

BLUNTISHAM

The High Street containing several elegant buildings, including the rebuilt Meeting House (1874) used by non-conformists since 1787 and the mid 18th-century farmhouse opposite. At the far end sited on the old green is the Barograph Memorial (1911). On the main road is the large former rectory (1720), once home of the writer Dorothy Sayers, some distance from the Parish Chuch of St Mary's with its unique 14th-century chancel which ends in three sides.

EARITH

Once a landing place for merchandise. Earith brought inland from the Wash and developed as an inland port for the timber trade. The Old and New Bedford Rivers built by Vermuyden in 1631 and 1651 respectively are drains that carry the Great Ouse to a sluice at Denver and eventually to the Wash. Close to the river Bridge is 'The Bulwark', as fortified earthworks built in the Civil War period. Locally, Earith is known as a venue for Fenland skating during the winter months, overlooked by the imposing church at Bluntisham perched on the side of a hill. After Earith, the Huntingdon district boundary is soon reached at the point where the River Ouse and the New Bedford River meet. On the south side of the Ouse are the villages of Willingham, Over, Swavesey and Fen Drayton, all of which are conservation areas around their historic centres.

Great Ouse Boating Association Limited

Affiliated to the Royal Yachting Association

GOBA, the Great Ouse Boating Association Limited, is registered under the Industrial and Provident Societies Acts. It is an association to which boat owners, boat clubs, boat builders, boat hirers and marina operators using the River Great Ouse and associated waterways are eligible to join.

By joining GOBA, you will help to ensure:

- continuation of navigation and mooring rights;
- adequate services at reasonable costs;
- a committee which will work on your behalf to solve what could become problems, often before you hear them.
- benefit free use of GOBA moorings.

Application for Membership of GOBA Ltd

Please complete in BLOCK LETTERS deleting inapplicable words

I/We wish to enrol as a Member(s) of the Great Ouse Boating Association Limited in accordance with the Association's Rules.

Title..

Address...

Name of Boat.. Reg No ....

My/our subscription will be paid by Bankers Order and the attached form has been completed, OR
My/our subscription for the current year is enclosed

Entrance fee	£2.00
Single £7.50 Joint £7.50	£............................
Please supply burgee @ £7.50	£............................
Please supply tie @ £6.50	£............................
Please supply ....badges @ £2.20 each	£............................
Total remittance, payable to GOBA Ltd, enclosed	£............................

Signed.. Date.......................................

Bankers Order (please do not detach from application form)
To .... Bank PLC
Branch address...
post code

Please pay to Barclays Bank PLC, St Ives Cambs (Code 20-43-63) for the account of the Great Ouse Boating Association Ltd Account No 00419753 the sum of £.......NOW and the sum of £...... on the 15th February annually until further notice commencing 15the February 19.....

Please debit my account name .... A/C No.

Signed.. Date ....

Address...
post code

Remitting Bank please quote Reference No
Membership applications to St Johns House,
High Street, Huntingdon